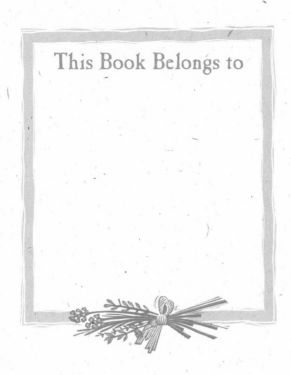

This Book Belongs to

*The mission of Storey Communications is to serve our customers
by publishing practical information that encourages personal independence
in harmony with the environment.*

Edited by Pamela Lappies
Cover and interior illustrations by Mary Rich
Cover and text design by Meredith Maker
Text production by Susan Bernier
Indexed by Northwind Editorial Services

Some recipes have been adapted from other Storey/Garden Way Publishing books: page 7: *The Pleasure of Herbs* by Phyllis V. Shaudys; pages 13, 14: *Satisfying Soups* by Phyllis Hobson; pages 24, 26: *Herbal Treasures* by Phyllis V. Shaudys; page 52: *The Joy of Gardening Cookbook* by Janet Ballantyne; page 60: *Tomatoes! 365 Healthy Recipes for Year-Round Enjoyment* by the Editors of Garden Way Publishing.

Printed in Canada by Métropole Litho

10 9 8 7 6 5 4 3 2 1

Library of Congress
Cataloging-in-Publication Data

Bass, Ruth, 1934–
    Tomatoes love herbs / Ruth Bass ;
        illustrations by Mary Rich.
        p.   cm.
    "A fresh from the garden cookbook."
    ISBN 0-88266-931-1 (hc : alk. paper)
    1. Cookery (Tomatoes) 2. Cookery
    (Herbs)   I. Title.
TX803.T6B36   1996
641.6'5642—dc20   96-10636
                                                CIP

TOMATOES LOVE HERBS

A
Fresh from the Garden
Cookbook

RUTH BASS

ILLUSTRATED BY MARY RICH

STOREY

A Storey Publishing Book
Storey Communications, Inc.

Introduction

Gertrude Stein would not have been able to deal with the tomato simply. If she had said, as she said of the rose, "A tomato is a tomato is a tomato," any gardener worth his or her trowel could debate the matter for hours.

It is all very well to plant the glamour pusses of the tomato world: the early females, the big males, the beefsteaks. Gardeners and cooks need tomatoes as soon as possible in the summer — that's why they sneak in one big plant that's already blooming — and everyone wants to produce a tomato that will more than cover a hamburger with a single slice.

But the tomato world is enormous, and the connoisseur learns that they not only don't look alike but don't taste alike, either. Pasta sauce is better if you have at least a few Italian plum-style tomatoes. For salads, the yellow pear shapes mix nicely with the red or pink cherry-type tomatoes. Tomatoes also come in egg shapes or fluted or striped in red and yellow, even in green and gold. Whatever their shape or color, their connection with herbs is like love and marriage in the old song — they go together.

Those who don't like the acidity of a regular tomato can choose low-acid yellow and orange ones, which make a nice color variation. Think of them side by side with the limey green of an avocado slice and its yellow lining. Think of them in a salad of crisp, fluffy leaf lettuce.

In addition to enjoying a wealth of spiffy hybrids, people are also looking back in time, just as they are seeking old-fashioned apples. Seeds can be found for heirloom tomatoes, one of the favorites being the Brandywine — pink-skinned, red inside, large, and of distinctive flavor.

Some tomatoes are better than others for canning or freezing. Some take to container gardening if your soil is in a pot next to the chaise on a patio. Some ripen more quickly than others. But all of them are enhanced with fresh herbs — especially basil, oregano, and dill. Don't ignore tomatoes with marjoram — cousin to oregano; tomatoes with fragrant thyme; memorable tomatoes with rosemary. And if fresh herbs are not available, just use dried — half or a third as much.

Garden tomatoes have one great disadvantage: They spoil you. After eating them every day from late July through late September — sometimes right in the garden, so warm that the juice just spills out and runs down your chin — you find you can't face even the most expensive ones offered in the supermarket. And you laugh at documentaries that explain how scientists are developing tomatoes that will be of uniform size, with skin tough enough for mechanical pickers and without too much juice — so they'll travel well. What the tomato lover wants is tender skin, plenty of juice, and the sweetness that comes from being ripened in the heat of the July and August sun.

When my brother-in-law, Harold, arrived at our house at the height of tomato season one summer, he could not tear himself away from the stove. He was living in the heart of

Tex-Mex country, where tomatoes go into almost everything. All his dishes, he said — which went from huevos rancheros for breakfast to four-alarm chili at dinner — were enhanced by the addition of New England tomatoes. He was up to his elbows for four days, and we gorged on our precious tomatoes in a half dozen new ways.

In my own family, garden tomatoes were on the table almost every day in late summer, sliced and dressed simply with sugar and cider vinegar, the sweet and sour never choking out the tomato flavor.

After shunning store tomatoes, we tend to plant too many in the spring, and tomatoes hog garden space. The year my husband tried what seemed to be all the varieties that existed, we had ninety-six plants. We've fought off any repetition of that act, but once we start reading and looking at the pictures, we have to summon some willpower or we will get pulled into tomatoland once again.

Still, it's a sweet place to be.

Tomato Omelette with Marjoram

You can cut cherry tomatoes in half, heat a little olive oil in a small skillet, and put them in cut side down; then serve them sprinkled with fresh marjoram next to eggs. Or you can turn out this omelette, which combines tomatoes, marjoram, and farmer cheese, which is slightly tart and crumbly.

2 tablespoons extra virgin olive oil	8 eggs
3 fresh ripe tomatoes, chopped	¼ cup water
3 large shallots, minced	Salt and freshly ground
1 cup farmer cheese, crumbled	black pepper
2 teaspoons minced fresh marjoram	4 tablespoons butter

1. Heat the oil in a skillet. Add the tomatoes and shallots and cook until soft, stirring frequently. Remove the pan from the heat and stir in the cheese and marjoram. Set aside.

2. Beat the eggs with a fork until they are light and well-blended. Add the water plus salt and pepper to taste.

3. Melt the butter in a clean skillet; when it is hot and foamy, pour in the egg mixture. Cook until set, lifting the edge occasionally to let the liquid run under the cooked portion.

4. Spoon the tomato mixture across the middle of the omelet. Fold the sides toward the middle and let cook another minute or so.

4 SERVINGS

Tomato Pesto Frittata

Omelettes are fun, versatile, and tasty. Frittatas are elegant. You pull that puffed-up, golden dish out of the oven, and oohs and aahs are yours. For a special breakfast or a quick but out-of-the-ordinary supper, put this frittata with pesto together in a very few minutes.

4 tablespoons extra virgin olive oil
2 onions, sliced
Salt
3 ripe tomatoes, peeled, seeded, and chopped
1 garlic clove, minced
5 eggs
Freshly ground black pepper
2 tablespoons chopped fresh basil
¼ cup chopped fresh parsley
2 tablespoons grated Parmesan cheese
1 teaspoon finely chopped pine nuts
2 tablespoons butter

1. In a large skillet, heat the oil and add the onions and a little salt. Cover the pan and simmer over low heat for 5 minutes. Uncover and cook until soft and golden.

2. Add the tomatoes and minced garlic, stirring to coat all ingredients. Let simmer for 15 minutes, then drain off the oil. Set the vegetables aside.

3. Preheat the oven to 350°F. In a large bowl, beat the eggs and add the tomato and onion mixture, pepper to taste, basil, parsley, cheese, and pine nuts. Combine well.

4. Place the butter in a 10-inch layer cake pan and put it in the oven until the butter melts. Swirl the butter to cover the sides of the pan. Pour in the frittata mixture. Bake for about 15 minutes or until the eggs are no longer runny.

5. Loosen the edges and slide the frittata onto a serving plate, or serve from the pan, cutting pie-shaped pieces.

4 SERVINGS

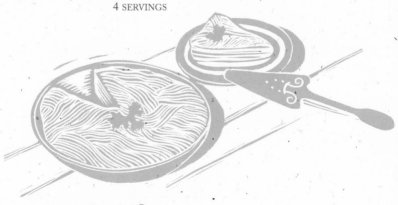

Sweet Million Appetizer

Sweet Million tomatoes were the next step after the Sweet 100s, gems in the world of what we generically refer to as cherry tomatoes. They grow in clusters like grapes, produce prolifically, and do not crack in late season the way some of their cousins do. They are pretty and tasty as a quick hors d'oeuvre or salad, especially when accompanied by fragrant basil.

> 1 quart Sweet Millions, or other cherry tomato
> 5 large basil leaves
> ¼ pound fresh mozzarella
> Freshly ground black pepper
> 1 sprig parsley
> Extra virgin olive oil

1. Wash the tomatoes, pat them dry, and slice off the stem ends.
2. Arrange the tomatoes on an attractive plate and put a snip of basil on each one.
3. Slice the mozzarella ¼-inch thick and cut into squares smaller than the tomatoes. Place a square on each tomato.
4. Top with a bit of pepper to taste and a bit of the parsley sprig. Add another small square of mozzarella and another bit of pepper and parsley. Drizzle the oil over the whole plate and let stand for at least a half hour before serving at room temperature.

4 SERVINGS AS A SALAD, 8 AS AN HORS D'OEUVRE

*Also called St. Josephwort, basil is held
in high esteem in the East but is regarded
as an agent of evil in Crete.*

Tomato Thyme Cocktail

This is one of those recipes that seems simple but delivers the goods. Ordinary tomato juice doesn't quite cut it after you've tried this version with thyme, which comes from Grandma's cookbook. You can cook up as many tomatoes as you want if you're willing to can the juice.

3–4 pounds ripe tomatoes
2 teaspoons chopped fresh thyme, or 1 teaspoon dried
Juice of 1½ lemons
1 teaspoon salt
½ cup sugar
Pinch of ground cloves

1. Cut up the tomatoes. In a large enameled or stainless-steel kettle, combine the tomatoes and the thyme. Heat them to boiling and cook gently until soft.
2. Put the cooked tomatoes through a food mill to remove the bulky part of the pulp. Then put the mixture through a large strainer to remove all seeds and pulp.
3. Add the lemon juice, salt, sugar, and cloves. Chill before serving.

1 QUART

Tomato, Basil, and Barley Soup

The sweetness of tomatoes with the heartiness of barley makes a filling soup for a winter day. This one adds the flavor of basil and will take care of a small crowd, so put it in a ceramic pot and keep it hot on a warming tray.

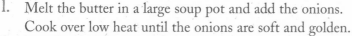

4 tablespoons softened butter
2 medium sweet onions, chopped
2 quarts water
8 medium tomatoes, peeled and chopped (4 cups)
1 cup barley
1 large garlic clove on a toothpick
2 tablespoons chopped fresh basil
Salt and freshly ground pepper

1. Melt the butter in a large soup pot and add the onions. Cook over low heat until the onions are soft and golden.
2. Fill another pot with the water and bring to a boil. Drop the tomatoes in and remove after a few seconds, reserving the boiling water. Rinse the tomatoes with cold water and peel. Add to the onions the tomatoes, boiling water, barley, garlic, and basil.
3. Simmer, covered, for 1–1½ hours. Remove the garlic, add salt and pepper to taste, and serve.

3 QUARTS

Parsleyed Tomato Bisque

Tomato soup is ubiquitous. From the Campbell's every American kid has enjoyed with a grilled-cheese sandwich to versions found in far-off lands, it warms us. This version marries tomatoes with bay leaves and parsley.

>   8   *tomatoes, chopped (2½ cups)*
>   1   *teaspoon sugar*
>   1   *cup water*
>   1   *sweet white onion, chopped*
>   3   *tablespoons softened butter*
>   2   *garlic cloves, put through a press*
>   1   *bay leaf*
> ½   *cup chopped fresh parsley*
>   3   *slices crusty Italian bread*
>   4   *cups low-fat milk*
>   *Salt and freshly ground black pepper*

1. In a large soup pot, cook the tomatoes and sugar in the water at medium heat for 20 minutes or until the tomatoes are soft.
2. In a separate pan, cook the onion in the butter until it is soft and golden, not browned. Add to the soup pot, along with the garlic, bay leaf, and parsley. Cook at medium heat for 5 minutes. Remove the bay leaf.

3. Using a blender or food processor, make fine bread crumbs from the crusty bread. You should have about 1 cup. Set aside. Then, in the same container, puree the soup mixture and return to the pot.
4. Combine the bread crumbs and milk in a separate saucepan, and heat to the scalding point (when the milk will just start to skin over). Add the milk and crumbs to the soup pot, stir well, and reheat to the boiling point.
5. Add salt and pepper to taste, and serve in heated bowls.

6 SERVINGS

Andalusian Gazpacho

Those who cheered on the world's athletes at the 1992 Olympic Games discovered a special treat at the sidewalk cafés of Barcelona: a silky smooth gazpacho that was cold, refreshing, and almost the color of cream of tomato soup. Here's how they made it:

3 garlic cloves
3 slices white bread
2 green peppers
6–9 tomatoes (about 3 pounds)
6 tablespoons white wine vinegar
5 tablespoons olive oil
Salt and freshly ground black pepper
A dash of sugar
1 cucumber
1 onion
1 red pepper
¼ cup chopped fresh chervil

1. Mash the garlic cloves. Remove the crusts from the bread and cut into cubes. Chop one of the peppers, and peel the tomatoes. Cut 2 slices from one of the tomatoes and reserve.

2. Put the garlic, bread, chopped pepper, tomatoes, vinegar, oil, salt and pepper to taste, and sugar in a food processor or blender and give it a whirl. If the mixture seems thick, add a little cold water to make it soupy. Chill.

3. Finely dice the cucumber, onion, red and green peppers, the chervil, and the 2 reserved slices of tomato. Put each into a separate serving bowl.

4. Put a couple of ice cubes in chilled soup cups, and pour the soup over. Garnish with the diced vegetables.

6 SERVINGS

Dilly Tomatoes

You think: tomatoes and basil. No, tomatoes and oregano. No, tomatoes and parsley. Ah, but then there's tomatoes and dill. It appears that the tomato, lushest of the garden vegetables, can cozy up to any one of the herbs — or several at once.

4 *large ripe tomatoes*
½ *cup plain yogurt*
2 *tablespoons snipped fresh dillweed*
¼ *cup mayonnaise*
1 *scallion, minced (2 tablespoons)*
Salt and freshly ground pepper
1 *garlic clove, minced*
2 *tablespoons butter*

1. Preheat the broiler. Core the tomatoes and remove a thin slice from the blossom end.
2. Combine the yogurt, dill, mayonnaise, scallion, and a little salt. Refrigerate the mixture.
3. Cut the tomatoes in half, crosswise. Place them on a broiling pan cut side up and season with the minced garlic and the salt and pepper to taste. Dot with the butter.

4. Broil 3 inches from the heat for 5 minutes or until the tomatoes are heated through.
5. To serve, top with the chilled yogurt mixture.

Dill derives its name from the Norse word dilla, *which means "to lull."*

Tomato Bean Blend with Thyme

Black and red make a stunning salad combination, especially if the vegetables are arranged on a black dish and sprinkled with herbs. This should be prepared in a serving dish no more than 10 inches in diameter so that you'll have a number of layers, and the flavors will blend.

2 large red bell peppers
8 medium tomatoes
½ cup sun-dried tomatoes in olive oil
3 tablespoons minced fresh parsley
2 tablespoons minced fresh thyme
2 tablespoons minced fresh oregano

⅔ cup fine, unflavored bread crumbs
1½ tablespoons grated Romano cheese
4 tablespoons extra virgin olive oil
1½ teaspoons white wine vinegar
1 can (16 ounces) black beans
Salt and freshly ground black pepper
1 tablespoon capers

1. Preheat the broiler. Slice the red peppers lengthwise, removing stem and seeds. Place the peppers skin side up on a broiling pan, and pop under the broiler for 5 to 7 minutes, charring them.

2. Place the blackened peppers in a paper bag, close it tightly, and set aside for 10 minutes.

3. In the meantime, set the oven at 375°F. Remove the stem and blossom ends from the tomatoes and cut into ¼-inch slices. Drain the sun-dried tomatoes and finely chop. Combine the parsley, thyme, and oregano in a small bowl. Combine the bread crumbs and cheese in a separate bowl.

4. Open the bag of peppers, taking care not to get burned on escaping steam. When they are cool enough to handle, peel the peppers and slice into strips.

5. Mix the oil and vinegar, and pour half the mixture into a bake-and-serve dish. Add a layer of tomatoes and a thin layer of black beans. Sprinkle with some of the sun-dried tomatoes, herb mixture, and pepper to taste.

6. Add a layer of pepper strips. Cover them with more tomato slices, beans, sun-dried tomatoes, herbs, pepper, and salt to taste. Continue until all the vegetables have been used. Pour the rest of the oil and vinegar over the top; add the capers and the bread crumb mixture. Bake 30 minutes or until the top is browned and the tomatoes are soft.

7. Cool on the counter, and then refrigerate. Serve chilled.

4 SERVINGS

Green Beans with Tomatoes and Savory

If the garden behaves nicely and produces slender, crisp green beans just as the tomatoes are becoming fat and red, this salad with parsley and savory will be very special. It can be served at room temperature or well chilled.

About a pound of green beans
4 medium tomatoes
1 small sweet onion, chopped
4 tablespoons extra virgin olive oil
Juice of half a large lemon
1 garlic clove, minced
½ cup chopped fresh parsley
2 tablespoons chopped fresh savory
3 tablespoons pine nuts
Salt and freshly ground pepper

1. Fill a pot with water and bring to a boil. Meanwhile, snip the ends off the beans, but leave them whole. When the water is boiling, drop the tomatoes in for a few seconds, remove, then rinse with cold water and peel. Chop and place in a strainer to let some of the juice run off.
2. Combine the onion, oil, lemon juice, garlic, parsley, savory, and pine nuts in a small jar with a tightly fitting lid. Shake well; then let stand.

3. Cook the beans about 5 minutes over medium heat in a saucepan with water to cover. They should be crisp. Drain, rinse with cold water to stop the cooking, and drain again.
4. Place the beans and tomatoes in a salad bowl. Pour the dressing mixture over the vegetables and toss gently. The flavors should be allowed to blend for at least 15 minutes before serving.
5. Serve at room temperature or chilled.

6 SALAD SERVINGS

Marinated Vegetables with Tarragon

When the produce looks picture-perfect in either the garden or the supermarket, vegetables need no cooking. Don't boil — marinate. Almost any vegetable you like can be substituted in this dish: Try slim slices of red onion, zucchini, or cauliflower, for instance.

¾ cup extra virgin olive oil
½ cup rosemary or tarragon vinegar
2 tablespoons lemon juice
4 tablespoons chopped scallions, green and white parts
2 teaspoons minced fresh tarragon
Salt and freshly ground pepper

2 teaspoons sugar
2 medium tomatoes, chopped (1 cup)
1 cup halved cherry tomatoes
1 cup pea pods, trimmed
1 cup coarsely chopped unpeeled zucchini

1. In a medium bowl, whisk together the oil, vinegar, lemon juice, scallions, tarragon, salt and pepper to taste, and sugar.
2. Arrange the tomatoes, pea pods, and zucchini in a shallow dish and add the marinade. Cover with plastic wrap and refrigerate for 3 to 24 hours. Stir at least once.
3. Drain off the marinade before serving.

4–6 SERVINGS

Rosemary or Tarragon Vinegar

This recipe, taken from *Herbal Vinegar* by Maggie Oster, can be adapted for use with any herb.

> *1 cup loosely packed fresh rosemary or tarragon leaves*
> *2 cups sherry vinegar or white wine vinegar*

1. Place the herbs in a clean, sterilized jar and use a spoon to bruise them slightly. Pour the vinegar over the herbs and cover the jar tightly.
2. Put the jar in a dark place at room temperature to let the herb-vinegar mixture steep. Shake the jar every few days and taste the vinegar after a week. If the flavor is not strong enough, let it stand for another 1 to 3 weeks, checking the flavor weekly. If an even stronger flavor is desired, repeat the steeping process with fresh herbs.
3. When the flavor is right, strain the vinegar, fill a clean, sterilized bottle, cap tightly, and label.

2 CUPS

Herbed Tomatoes with Avocados

These tomatoes blend with herbs to make an ideal buffet dish that can be made a day ahead of time. Well in advance, buy the dark-skinned avocados for this dish. Few things are less flavorful than a not-ready avocado.

> 10 *avocados, peeled and cut into chunks*
> *Juice of half a lemon*
> 1 *large jar (64 ounces) of artichoke hearts, including liquid*
> 4 *large tomatoes, chopped coarsely*
> 5 *stalks of celery, chopped, including leaves*
> 2 *cups chopped onion*
> ½ *cup sun-dried tomatoes*
> 3 *tablespoons chopped chives*
> 2 *garlic cloves, minced*
> 2 *tablespoons chopped fresh tarragon*
> 1 *teaspoon chopped fresh thyme*

1. Place the avocado chunks in a large bowl and toss with the lemon juice.
2. Add the artichokes and liquid, tomatoes, celery, onion, sun-dried tomatoes, chives, garlic, tarragon, and thyme. Toss gently, cover with plastic wrap, and refrigerate for up to 24 hours.
3. Drain liquid before serving.

ABOUT 6 QUARTS OF VEGETABLES

Tarragon Tomato Salad Dressing

If you make your own French-style dressing, it will taste fresh and perhaps carry fewer calories to the salad. You can substitute basil, oregano, thyme, or chervil for the tarragon.

> ¾ cup tomato juice
> ¼ cup white wine vinegar
> ½ cup yogurt
> 1 tablespoon Worcestershire sauce
> 1 scallion, chopped
> 1 tablespoon minced fresh tarragon
> ¼ teaspoon prepared mustard
> Freshly ground pepper

1. Combine the juice, vinegar, yogurt, Worcestershire, scallion, tarragon, mustard, and pepper to taste, in a blender and process until smooth. Refrigerate for an hour so that the flavors will blend.
2. To store, refrigerate in a tightly covered container.

1¾ CUPS

Stuffed Tomatoes Niçoise

If it says *Niçoise* (knee-SWAHZ), it's bound to have black olives and garlic and olive oil and anchovies. This recipe has all those things and more.

6 large tomatoes
2 tablespoons olive oil
6 shallots, chopped
1 tablespoon anchovy paste or mashed anchovies
2 tablespoons chopped black olives
1 tablespoon chopped fresh basil
1 garlic clove, minced
2 tablespoons chopped fresh parsley
1 teaspoon capers, chopped
Salt and freshly ground pepper
1 can (7 ounces) white-meat tuna
¼ cup dry white wine
1 cup cooked pastini or orzo
   (½ cup uncooked)
¼ cup fine bread crumbs
1 tablespoon butter

1. Preheat the oven to 400°F. Slice the tops off the tomatoes and hollow them out, reserving the pulp. Chop the pulp.
2. Heat the oil in a pan, add the shallots, and cook until they are golden. Stir in the tomato pulp, anchovy paste, olives, basil, garlic, parsley, capers, and salt and pepper to taste. Flake the tuna and add to the mixture. Blend in the wine.
3. Cook for 2 minutes; then add the cooked pasta. Fill the tomatoes with the mixture. Top with bread crumbs and dot with butter.
4. Bake about 15 minutes, or until the tomatoes are cooked through.

6 SERVINGS

Ancient Romans and Greeks believed
that wearing garlands of parsley
would prevent drunkenness.

Not-So-Welsh Rarebit

Commonly called "rabbit," the rarebit is usually a somewhat sharp, cheesy concoction served on toast for lunch or a simple supper. This one includes parsley, tomatoes, and a Texas-style whammy.

4 large ripe tomatoes
2 medium onions
1 medium green pepper, seeded
¾ teaspoon cayenne
A few drops of hot chili oil
2 tablespoons butter
1 cup cubed sharp cheddar cheese
1 tablespoon minced fresh parsley and sprigs for garnish
1 teaspoon mustard
1 teaspoon Worcestershire sauce
½ cup milk
Sourdough or Italian bread

1. Fill a pot with water and bring to a boil. Drop the tomatoes in for less than a minute, remove, rinse with cold water, peel, and chop. Chop the onions and pepper.

2. In a saucepan, combine the tomatoes, onions, pepper, cayenne, and hot chili oil. Cook over medium heat for about 30 minutes. If the tomatoes are very

juicy, drain off most of the liquid. Let the mixture cool before making the cheese sauce.

3. In a double boiler, melt the butter, add the cheese, and stir until the cheese has melted. Add the parsley, mustard, Worcestershire sauce, and milk.

4. Cook, stirring frequently, until thickened. Then add the tomato sauce and reheat. Serve hot on toasted sourdough or crisp Italian bread. Garnish with parsley sprigs.

4 TO 6 SERVINGS

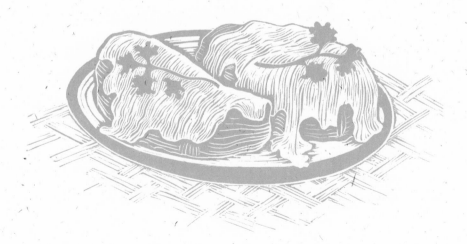

Tomato Basil Bake

Vegetarians can make a meal out of this. It's also a perfect accompaniment to a simple chicken or veal dish, providing vegetables and potatoes in one casserole, blended with basil.

5 tablespoons *extra virgin olive oil*
3 *ripe but firm tomatoes*
6 *medium potatoes*
3 *sweet onions, sliced paper-thin (2 cups)*
¼ *cup minced fresh basil*
2 *garlic cloves, minced*
Salt and freshly ground pepper
½ *cup grated Parmesan cheese*
¼ *cup grated Romano cheese*
½ *cup water*

1. Preheat the oven to 400°F, and lightly grease a 13 x 9-inch baking dish with 1 tablespoon of the oil.
2. Fill a pot with water and bring to a boil. Drop the tomatoes in for less than a minute, remove, rinse with cold water, and peel. Dice them, removing most of the seeds. Peel the potatoes and slice them ¼-inch thick.

3. In a bowl, combine the remaining oil, onion, tomato, basil, garlic, salt and pepper to taste, and grated cheeses. Mix in the water. Add the potatoes and toss to mix well.
4. Put the mixture in the baking dish and bake on an upper shelf of the oven for an hour, or until the potatoes are done. The mixture should be stirred after 20 minutes and again after another 20 minutes.

6 SERVINGS

Basil derives its name from the Greek word basileus, *which means "king."*

Creamy Tomato Sauce with Herbs

If you have leftover chicken or turkey, or you'd like to give your tuna casserole a change of direction, substitute this herbed sauce for a plain white sauce. You could also use it over vegetables, such as fresh asparagus on toast.

> 2 tablespoons butter
> 2 tablespoons flour
> 1 cup milk, at room temperature
> ½ teaspoon salt
> Freshly ground pepper
> 2 large ripe tomatoes, chopped (about 2 cups)
> 1 sweet onion, minced
> 1 tablespoon minced fresh basil
> 1 teaspoon minced fresh parsley
> ¼ teaspoon minced fresh thyme
> 2 garlic cloves, minced

1. In the microwave, melt the butter in a quart-size glass measuring cup or other container tall enough to keep the butter from splattering.
2. Stir in the flour, and microwave for 2 minutes, stirring after the first minute.
3. Add the milk slowly, stirring continuously. Microwave for 4 minutes, stirring after each minute. Stir in the salt, and add pepper to taste. Set aside.

4. Start over low heat, cook the tomatoes and onion for about 10 minutes. Add the basil, parsley, thyme, and garlic, and simmer another 2 minutes.
5. Puree the tomato mixture in a blender or food processor, and combine with the white sauce.

ABOUT 3 CUPS

Red Sauce with Basil for Pasta

Tomato sauce comes in a thousand guises. With most of the recipes, you can add or subtract ingredients to get the perfect blend. This one provides a start, and the result can be used on spaghetti or in lasagna. Sauteed ground beef can be added to make a meat sauce, and other herbs can be added. The sauce also freezes beautifully for winter use. If it's a little watery — sometimes a tomato can be too juicy — add a can of tomato paste.

¼ cup butter
¼ cup extra virgin olive oil
2 onions, coarsely chopped
4 garlic cloves, chopped
¼ cup chopped fresh parsley
4 pounds ripe tomatoes
1 stalk celery with leaves
¼ cup basil leaves, packed
Salt and freshly ground pepper

1. In a large saucepan, melt the butter, add the oil, and sauté the onions until they are golden but not browned. Stir in the garlic and parsley, and cook over low heat for 3 minutes.
2. Put the tomatoes, celery, and basil in a food processor or blender and puree. Add salt and pepper to taste. Pour into the saucepan, and cook slowly for at least 2 hours.
3. If you like a chunky sauce, serve it as is. If you prefer smooth, put it through a blender or a food mill.

2 QUARTS

*High in chlorophyll, parsley leaves
are natural breath fresheners.*

Pesto Tomato Pasta

The green sauce — with basil as the major ingredient — has become a staple for American cooks. Here it combines with summer's best tomatoes and rotelle for a taste treat.

> ¾ cup extra virgin olive oil
> ½ cup balsamic vinegar
> 2 cups fresh basil leaves
> ½ cup fresh parsley
> 4 large garlic cloves
> Salt and freshly ground pepper
> 8 large tomatoes, peeled and cut into quarters
> 1 pound rotelle or other pasta
> ½ cup grated Parmesan cheese

1. Put a large pot of water on the stove to boil.
2. Place the oil and vinegar in a food processor, and add the basil, parsley, garlic, and salt and pepper to taste. Puree.
3. Add the tomatoes, and process until they are coarsely chopped. Refrigerate the mixture.

4. Cook the pasta in boiling water according to the directions on the package. Drain.
5. While the pasta is hot, add the tomato mixture and toss gently. Serve immediately with Parmesan cheese while the pasta is still warm.

6 TO 8 SERVINGS

Herbed Spaghetti Sauce in the Raw

An elegant way to prepare spaghetti sauce when tomatoes are red and lush and sweet at midsummer is not to cook the sauce at all. Just add fresh herbs and serve.

> 2 pounds fresh, really ripe tomatoes
> 1 pound linguini or other spaghetti
> 2 garlic cloves, minced
> ½ cup fresh basil leaves, packed
> 3 tablespoons finely chopped fresh parsley
> ¼ cup extra virgin olive oil
> Juice of 1 lemon
> Salt and freshly ground pepper
> ¼ cup grated Parmesan
> ¼ cup grated Romano

1. The tomatoes should be at room temperature, neither hot from the garden nor chilled. Chop them, then place in a strainer. Let drain for at least 15 minutes.

2. In a large pot, drop the linguini into boiling water and make sure the strands are separated. Cook according to taste or the directions on the package.

3. Cut the basil leaves into short strips. Place the tomatoes in a bowl, add the garlic, basil, parsley, oil, and lemon juice, and toss gently. Add salt and pepper to taste.
4. Drain the linguini, place in warmed pasta bowl, pour the sauce over the top, and mix lightly. Serve with the grated cheeses.

4 SERVINGS

41

Spicy Green Tomato Bread

Those who live where frost pounces suddenly in the fall often mourn the loss of all those glossy, green tomatoes that won't get time to ripen. Or, they can harvest a bushel or two and cook them up with oregano and spices.

2 ¼ cups unbleached white flour
1 ½ teaspoons baking powder
1 teaspoon baking soda
¼ teaspoon salt
¼ teaspoon ground nutmeg
1 teaspoon ground ginger
1 tablespoon minced fresh oregano
2 eggs
⅓ cup honey
⅓ cup melted, unsalted butter
⅔ cup apple cider (preferably without preservatives)
2–3 green tomatoes, diced (1–1 ¼ cups)

1. Preheat the oven to 325°F, and butter a large loaf pan. Sift the flour, baking powder, soda, salt, nutmeg, ginger, and oregano together.
2. In a large bowl, beat the eggs, add the honey, and beat again; then add the butter and cider, and keep beating. Stir in the tomatoes.

3. Fold in the dry ingredients until everything is combined. Pour the batter into the greased pan, and bake about an hour, or until the top springs back when touched and the edges are pulling away from the sides of the pan.
4. Cool on a rack for 10 minutes in the pan. Then remove from pan to cool completely on the rack.

1 LOAF

Cilantro Tomato Sandwich

BLT's are melt-in-your-mouth sandwiches when they're made with garden tomatoes. It's the one time of the year that my family splurges on bacon. This cheesy, spiky version with cilantro and without lettuce is delicious, too.

> 3 tablespoons mayonnaise
> 1 teaspoon chili powder
> 4 ounces shredded cheddar cheese
> 4 slices rye bread
> 4 slices crisply cooked bacon
> 2 medium tomatoes, sliced
> 2 tablespoons minced fresh cilantro
> Olive oil

1. Combine the mayonnaise, chili powder, and cheese, and spread on 2 slices of the bread.
2. Add the bacon and the tomato slices and sprinkle with the cilantro. Add the second slice to each sandwich.
3. Wipe the surface of a large skillet with a little olive oil, and heat the skillet. Add the sandwiches, cooking 3 to 4 minutes a side and taking great care not to lose the contents when turning.

2 SANDWICHES

Herbed Tomato Preserves

Here's a recipe that uses the smaller tomatoes in your garden.

1 teaspoon snipped fresh dill
1 bay leaf, crushed or snipped finely
1 teaspoon coriander seed
½ teaspoon allspice
½ teaspoon mustard seed
1-inch piece of ginger root, peeled

4 cups sugar
2 lemons, sliced thinly
¾ cup water
1½ quarts small red tomatoes, peeled (8 pounds)

1. Tie the herbs, spices, and ginger root in cheesecloth. Put in a large pot with the sugar, lemon slices, and water, and simmer for 15 minutes.
2. Add the tomatoes and cook gently until almost transparent, stirring occasionally. Cover and let stand in a cool place for 12 to 18 hours.
3. Scrub 6 half-pint canning jars with two-piece lids. Boil the lids gently for 5 minutes and leave in the hot water.
4. Heat the tomato mixture to a boil. With a slotted spoon, scoop the mixture into the hot canning jars, leaving ½-inch of space at the top.
5. Remove the herb-and-spice bag. Boil the remaining syrup for 2 to 3 minutes, longer if it seems really watery. Pour the boiling hot syrup over the tomatoes, but not above the ½-inch point. Put on the lids and rings and process in a boiling water bath for 20 minutes.

6 HALF PINTS

Green Tomato Dill Pickle

In a year when frost comes long before the tomatoes have all ripened, it's time to make this pickle, which is both sweet and sharp and makes a beautiful addition to a Christmas basket of homemade goodies. While it's meant as a condiment, it can also be enjoyed as a sandwich filling.

¼ cup coarse salt
5 pounds green tomatoes, thinly sliced
½ pound onions, thinly sliced
4 teaspoons snipped fresh dillweed
½ teaspoon whole allspice
½ teaspoon whole cloves
½ teaspoon celery seed
1 large red pepper, chopped
1½ cups cider vinegar
¼ lemon, thinly sliced
½ tablespoon dry mustard
1½ cups granulated sugar
4 flower heads of dill

1. In a large kettle, add the salt to the tomatoes and onions and mix thoroughly. Let stand in a cool place for 10 hours minimum or overnight. Drain.

2. Place the herb and the spices in a cheesecloth bag. Combine the pepper, vinegar, lemon slices, mustard, and sugar with the tomatoes and onions, and heat to a boil. Add the spice-and-herb bag, and boil slowly for a half hour, stirring frequently.
3. Place one dill flower head in each of 4 clean, dry canning jars.
4. Remove the spice-and-herb bag, and pour the tomato mixture into the jars. Seal and process in a pressure canner according to canner directions.
5. Remove jars, check seal a few hours later, and store.

4 PINTS

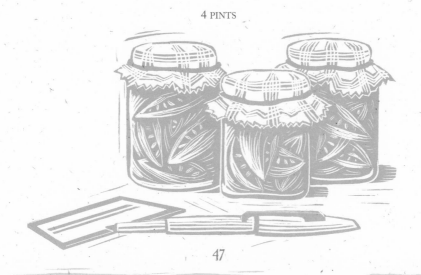

Fried Green Tomatoes

You probably saw the movie. Perhaps that led you to the book. The innovative restaurateurs of fiction had their Fried Green Tomatoes Restaurant and a recipe of the same name. This is different (minus the bacon drippings and with the addition of cilantro and oregano), but still delicious — and works for breakfast, lunch, or dinner.

> 4 *medium green tomatoes*
> 3 *tablespoons flour*
> 1 *teaspoon minced fresh cilantro*
> 1 *tablespoon minced fresh oregano*
> 1 *egg*
> 6 *tablespoons bread crumbs*
> 3 *tablespoons extra virgin*
> *olive oil*

1. Slice the unpeeled tomatoes and place in a single layer on several thicknesses of paper towels. Let stand while preparing the herbs and dips.
2. In a shallow bowl or pie pan, combine the flour with the cilantro and oregano. In a separate bowl, beat the egg. Have the bread crumbs ready in another pie pan.
3. Heat the oil in a large skillet. Dip the tomato slices in the flour mixture, then into the egg, and then into the bread crumbs. Sauté in the skillet until browned; turn and cook until tender. Add olive oil as necessary.

6 SERVINGS

Stuffed Tomatoes Oregano

You can put nearly anything into a tomato once you've hollowed it out: tuna fish, chopped mushrooms with parsley and garlic, crab meat with mayonnaise, chopped avocado with lemon juice. Here's one tasty idea with a seafood theme.

1 pound small cooked shrimp, deveined and rinsed
1 teaspoon minced fresh oregano
2 teaspoons minced fresh parsley
8 Greek-style olives, pitted and chopped
½ cup extra virgin olive oil
1½ tablespoons finely chopped scallions, green
   and white parts
Juice of 1 lemon
Salt and freshly ground black pepper
4 large ripe, firm tomatoes
4 curly lettuce leaves

1. Cut the shrimp into small pieces, and combine with the oregano, parsley, olives, oil, scallions, lemon juice, and salt and pepper to taste. Mix well, and set aside to let the flavors blend.
2. Cut a slice from the top of each tomato and a slim slice from the blossom end. Scoop out the pulp, and place the tomato on a leaf of lettuce. Fill with the shrimp mixture, and chill well before serving.

4 SERVINGS

Oregano gets its name from the Greek word origanum, *which means "joy of the mountains."*

Tarragon Chicken and Tomatoes

Marinating chicken lets the flavors of fresh herbs and freshly picked produce absorb right into the meat and assures tenderness, as well. This marinade doubles as a sauce.

3 large boneless chicken breasts, cut in half
8 tomatoes, peeled and chopped (4 cups)
1 leek, chopped
4 garlic cloves, minced
2 scallions cut into 1-inch pieces, green and white parts
1 tablespoon minced fresh parsley
3 teaspoons minced fresh tarragon
2 tablespoons light soy sauce
1 cup chicken broth
1 cup white wine
Salt and freshly ground black pepper

1. Carefully wash the chicken, and remove all fat and membranes. Drain on paper towels, and place in a single layer in a baking dish.
2. In a large bowl, combine the tomatoes, leek, garlic, scallions, parsley, tarragon, soy sauce, broth, wine, and salt and pepper to taste. Pour over the chicken. Cover tightly, and refrigerate for at least 2 hours or as long as overnight, turning the chicken a few times.

3. Preheat the oven to 350°F. Pour off the marinade into a skillet, and cook it down to about half its original volume. Pour the reduced sauce over the chicken, and bake for 30 minutes, uncovering for the last 15 minutes.

6 SERVINGS

Veal with Tomatoes and Oregano

When veal scallopini is pale in color and pounded very thin, it cooks quickly and marvelously. Tomatoes, delicate but flavorful in the vegetable world, are an excellent companion for veal. (If you can't find plum tomatoes, try another kind.)

1 tablespoon butter
1½ tablespoons extra virgin olive oil
3 garlic cloves
3–4 tablespoons flour
Salt and freshly ground black pepper
1 pound veal scallopini
½ cup dry white wine
3 ripe plum tomatoes, enough to make ½ cup
1 tablespoon chopped fresh oregano
2 tablespoons minced fresh parsley
2 tablespoons chopped black olives

1. Melt the butter in a large skillet and add the oil. When it is hot, sauté the garlic cloves whole until they are browned. Remove the garlic and discard.
2. Place the flour and ¼ teaspoon salt in a pie plate. Stir in pepper to taste, and dredge the scallopini in the flour, shaking each piece to get rid of the excess.

With the heat turned to medium high, sauté the scallopini in the oil and butter, less than a minute a side. When the veal slices are cooked, transfer them to a warm plate and do another batch until all are finished.

3. In the same skillet, add the wine, and as it starts to bubble, scrape loose the bits of meat stuck to the pan. Add the chopped tomatoes, continuing to stir. Simmer about 15 minutes.

4. Return the scallopini to the pan, along with the oregano and parsley, and keep turning the slices until they are reheated. Add the black olives, and serve on a warm platter.

4 SERVINGS

Beef, Tomato, and Leek Stir-Fry

Take a look at any assortment of ethnic cookbooks: The tomato shows up everywhere. This recipe has some Chinese characteristics, including soy sauce, and calls for stir-frying, which means the contents of the pan must be quickly scooped and turned over and over, so nothing sticks and everything cooks.

2 leeks
2 white onions
1½ pounds sirloin tip beef
6 tomatoes
1 tablespoon sugar
½ inch fresh ginger root, shredded
Salt
1½ cups beef stock
½ cup sherry or Chinese rice wine
3 tablespoons peanut oil
1½ tablespoons peppercorns
4 garlic cloves, chopped
2 teaspoons minced fresh savory
2 tablespoons light soy sauce
3–4 drops hot chili oil
1 tablespoon cornstarch
½ cup minced fresh chervil
3–4 cups cooked rice

1. Fill a pot with water and heat on high. While you are waiting for it to boil, cut off the green section of the leeks and discard. Slice the leeks in half lengthwise and soak in a pan of cool water for 10 minutes to make sure they are grit free. Slice the onions thinly, and cube the beef.
2. Drop the tomatoes into the boiling water for 30 seconds, remove, rinse with cold water, and peel. Cut into quarters and sprinkle with the sugar. Remove the leeks from the water and slice into 1-inch pieces.
3. In a large saucepan or wok, combine the beef, onions, ginger, salt to taste, stock, and sherry or rice wine. Bring to a boil, reduce the heat, and simmer gently for about an hour, turning the contents every 15 minutes.
4. When the liquid has been reduced to a quarter of its original volume, remove the pan from the heat, and take out the beef with a slotted spoon.
5. In a large skillet, heat the peanut oil. When it is hot, add the beef and peppercorns, and stir-fry over high heat for 2 minutes. Add the leeks, garlic, savory, soy sauce, and hot chili oil, and stir-fry another 2 minutes.
6. Add the tomatoes, turning and stirring continuously for another minute over high heat.
7. Combine the cornstarch with 3 tablespoons of water, and add to the sauce in the wok or saucepan. Bring that to a boil, pour it over the beef and tomato mixture, and bring it to the bubbling point again. Add the chervil, toss, and serve with fluffy rice.

6 SERVINGS

Harold's Four-Alarm Chili

Sometimes chili con carne is a thick stew with beef, tomatoes, and beans. Sometimes it's Tex-Mex dynamite in a bowl. Harold's is the latter, made with chopped beef — he always insisted that purists don't use beans and don't use ground beef — fresh tomatoes, herbs, and jalapeños. It's hot and delicious. Make it in September, freeze it for December.

>   1 large onion, chopped
>   2 tablespoons olive or other vegetable oil
>   3 pounds lean beef, cut into very small cubes
>   3 garlic cloves, chopped
>   7 medium ripe tomatoes, chopped
>   2 teaspoons chopped fresh oregano
>   5 teaspoons chili powder
>   2 teaspoons paprika
>   3 jalapeños, chopped, including seeds
>   1 tablespoon cumin
>   2 teaspoons salt
>   3 cups cooked rice

1. In a Dutch oven, sauté the onion in the oil. Add the beef, and cook until it begins to brown, stirring constantly.

2. Add the garlic and tomatoes, stirring to combine. Then add the oregano, chili powder, paprika, jalapeños, cumin, and salt.
3. Bring just to a boil, stirring to be sure the mixture doesn't stick. Turn the heat down, and simmer for 2 or 3 hours, stirring occasionally. Serve in preheated bowls over about ¼ cup rice per person.

10 SERVINGS

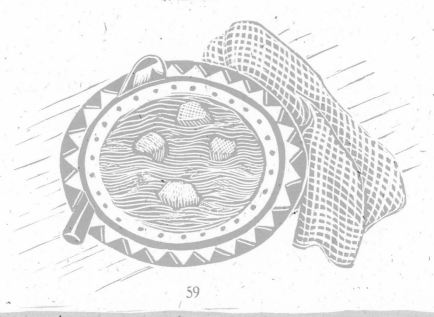

Green Tomato Crisp with Rosemary

You can serve tomatoes with every course, from appetizer to soup to entrée to dessert. And not just one dessert. There are cakes, green tomato pies, green tomato mincemeat pies, and this crunchy delight.

> 5 large green tomatoes
> ½ cup plus 2 tablespoons butter
> ½ teaspoon ginger
> 1 teaspoon cinnamon
> ¼ teaspoon nutmeg
> 1 tablespoon finely chopped fresh rosemary
> Zest of 1 large lemon
> 1 cup dark brown sugar
> 1 cup unflavored bread crumbs
> 1 cup wheat germ
> Juice of 1 large lemon

1. Preheat the oven to 350°F, and lightly oil a covered baking dish.
2. Wash the tomatoes and chop coarsely. Melt 2 tablespoons of the butter in a large saucepan, and add the tomatoes, spices, herb, and lemon zest. Add the brown sugar and stir well.
3. In a smaller pan, melt the remaining ½ cup butter, and add the bread crumbs and wheat germ.

4. Put half the crumb mixture in the baking dish, add the tomato mixture, and squeeze the lemon juice over it. Spread the rest of the crumb mixture over the top, cover, and bake 35 minutes. Remove the cover and bake another 10 minutes. Serve warm.

6 SERVINGS

Index

Converting Recipe Measurements to Metric

Use the following formulas for converting U.S. measurements to metric. Since the conversions are not exact, it's important to convert the measurements for all of the ingredients to maintain the same proportions as the original recipe.

When The Measurement Given Is	Multiply It By	To Convert To
teaspoons	4.93	milliliters
tablespoons	14.79	milliliters
fluid ounces	29.57	milliliters
cups (liquid)	236.59	milliliters
cups (liquid)	.236	liters
cups (dry)	275.31	milliliters
cups (dry)	.275	liters
pints (liquid)	473.18	milliliters
pints (liquid)	.473	liters
pints (dry)	550.61	milliliters
pints (dry)	.551	liters
quarts (liquid)	946.36	milliliters
quarts (liquid)	.946	liters
quarts (dry)	1101.22	milliliters
quarts (dry)	1.101	liters
gallons	3.785	liters
ounces	28.35	grams
pounds	.454	kilograms
inches	2.54	centimeters
degrees Fahrenheit	$5/9$ (temperature $- 32$)	degrees Celsius

While standard metric measurements for dry ingredients are given as units of mass, U.S. measurements are given as units of volume. Therefore, the conversions listed above for dry ingredients are given in the metric equivalent of volume.